D1264435

A WALK IN THE WOODS
By Marjolein Bastin

WRITTEN AND
ILLUSTRATED BY

Marjolein Bastin

DESIGNED BY

Helen Fahler

EDITED BY

Tara Pfeifer

MANUFACTURED FOR AND
© 1995 HALLMARK CARDS, INC.
KANSAS CITY, MO 64141

PRINTED IN HONG KONG
ASSEMBLED IN CHINA

Walking in nature is something we all can do to treat ourselves. When you are outside, all things come to you--you see, you hear, you touch and smell, you discover so many tiny and huge things!

For me, the sheltering woods are an extra-special place, full of life and excitement and wonder. I feel so happy when I'm there, like a child again, really! The chatter of birds, a busy squirrel building her nest, a young wood owl testing his wings, unexpected colors more beautiful than you can imagine... These are just a few of the many wonderful treasures nature freely shares with us.

I think walking in nature is one of the greatest feelings of completeness you can have. And when you leave the woods, you'll find yourself rich in the things that really count!

Marjolein Bastin

It's still a bit cold, but our bird friends already like the look of things! They've discovered a hole that's just the right size. The female flies in and out a few times with a satisfied look on her face. If I get too close, the male scolds and drives me away. A few weeks ago, he was happy to eat my peanuts...

For this pair, spring can begin! They have each
other, they have their eye on a nesting site, and
they're getting pretty fed up with winter food.
Without much success, they open a few more oak
apples. But most of the gall wasps have already
crawled out...

Angrily, they throw
the pieces over
their shoulders.

The fox sniffs the ground for signs of a rabbit or a mouse.

Hunger makes anything more appetizing...
"If necessary, some dung beetles, then. If I must!"

Here under the juneberry, the jays buried a bunch of acorns last fall. Now that they're hungry, they can find them without hesitation.

The male spotted woodpecker sends out a passionate drumming sound. He does this to attract the females and to mark his territory, keeping other males away. The female listens as she hangs on the trunk with interest.

Our woodpecker is quite inventive! In various places in his territory, he uses branches as his drumsticks, preferably dead ones which resonate nicely. He happily drums away... kind of like a private music concert. As the brooding season approaches, his drumrolls sound more regularly and last longer.

"Which is just his way of saying, "Welcome, Madame, you are hereby invited to my hideaway!"

This female squirrel devotes enormous energy to building the nest where she will soon raise her young. First she chased her mate away. Only in the beginning did he help drag branches. Apparently she prefers doing the finer work herself. Dozens of times, she runs back and forth, up and down.

She begins with clumps of dry grass...

later I see her pulling moss from the ground.

She doesn't even notice me. She's much too busy.

And here a nice bunch of lesser celandine,
which I've been anticipating for weeks.

It's a magical moment when a family of badgers show their black-and-white noses in the evening twilight.

A young wood owl learns to fly! Actually, he can really just flap about. He flounders around among the branches on the ground. Then the rabbit discovered him.

Carefully the owl was sniffed. Then I saw something really surprising... the rabbit jumped over him and kicked out toward his head. Poor little owl. Suddenly one of his parents took a dive and away ran the rabbit! The parent lured its offspring safely into the tr

The day is over. The evening sun shines over his head.
He looks like a sweet, angry little elf.

In a little bit, he'll
get a delicious mouse
from his parents.
He's earned it!

His first real day outside, and it was progress.
In the dark, I hear how he's being sumptuously fed.

This little one wriggles itself between mama's front legs for a cup of comfort... How sweet!

While their fathers and mothers are stretched out along the edge of the woods relaxing in the sun, the younger generations tirelessly romp around...

Sometimes they do a somersault right in the middle of a jump!

Wheee!!

Oh, no!

They scare the daylights out of the innocent green finches.

They run, jump, dive and all around have the time of their lives!

On another of my excursions,
I come across something so delicate...
a newly-born fawn. His mother has found
a safe nook where she's "parked" him
for a short while. He is so touchingly
beautiful, so vulnerable.

If you ever find a fawn like that,
leave it alone, don't touch it, and
disappear as quickly as possible.
The fawn waits motionlessly until
his mother comes to get him. She'll
only do that if she sees no people
or dogs anywhere in the vicinity.

What a commotion all of a sudden! Shrieking jays, grumbling blackbirds. I know immediately what's happening...they've discovered the sleeping quarters of an owl. When I appear on the scene, the smaller birds are just beginning to attack. The owl doesn't even budge, just casually blinks his big dark eyes. But his ears must be ringing! For years the owl couple have been living here in the woods, always true to each other and their territory. The wife sleeps in her own tree and the husband in a different spot every time, yet never far from her. Thanks to the ruckus out there, I now know exactly where.

This one is so furious that he breaks
branches off an adjacent tree and
throws them around. Vandalism?

I begin to get pretty attached to a drawing spot under the oak tree. Will I ever have to leave here?

I just held the funniest critter that I have ever seen...a spotted salamander. I found him near a little murmuring stream.

He loves moist places where he can hunt earthworms, snails and all kinds of insects.

And this little guy proves that wall lizards don't always reside in sun-drenched piles of stones. If he flashes away, at least I still have this beautiful old fence...

People who don't like pellets should quickly turn the page. But they'll be missing something! Pellets are really fascinating because they offer an expedition through the menus of several kinds of birds. They spit up, almost in the shape of balls, indigestible things like bones, hair or plastic.

OWL PELLETS

Owls' pellets are the most beautiful because their digestive juices aren't capable of dissolving even the littlest bone. By taking apart such a pellet and removing all the mouse hair, you get a well-preserved set of one or more mice. The whole layout below comes from a single pellet.

I've taken apart quite a few of them. In most, there are mice, the owl's main food source. But I also found the leftovers of a rat, a mole, a robin, a wren and even a crossbill!

This old pellet now serves as nourishing soil to little mushrooms.

Everything gets utilized in nature.

Through the early morning mist I spot a wild boar casually ambling down a wooded path. Then another one appears. And another. A little later...one more...and still another.

Five of them stand and look over at me, fifty feet away. This is a pack of females and adolescents. The males usually travel alone. They burrow for acorns, beech nuts, plant roots and anything else that happens to be in their path.

With my binoculars, I luxuriate in this picture.
What bristles and inquisitive, tiny eyes they have.
Mrs. Boar certainly has a charm of her own !!

My binoculars come in handy once again.
The black woodpecker looks so fantastic
with the sun on his flaming crest

He's chopping a nice stump to smithereens
because he knows what he can find there...
wonderful, tasty beetles and larvae!

It's very humid in the woodland meadow, to the great enjoyment of the snails.

I count 104 of them!

When I find their empty houses, I can't resist taking a few with me.

So many surprising colors...and such beauty in something so simple.

A hungry wren looks for little creatures living in the wall.

Everyone gets scared now!
But really, why? Just because
she happens to have eight legs
instead of two or four? Just
because she happens to have
eight eyes? Or six spinnerets?

True, you don't want her in your
clothes. And sticky cobwebs,
no matter how artfully woven, are
no fun to have across your face.
But spiders really are very helpful.
They catch the same many-footed
creatures that we fanatically chase
with the flyswatter!

And they also participate quite actively in recycling.
Old spider webs are not simply tossed out into the street...
Oh no, they eat them in order to make new ones.
A better environment begins with yourself!

Many toadstools profit from someone else...
sometimes with death as the result.

Like the honey fungus. When these bunches appear on the trunk of a healthy tree, it will not live much longer.

Another dangerous parasite is the pine killer. Its name says it all.

A bit smaller, but just as fatal, is a caterpillar-eating toadstool called a "Grainy Club." Every fall, dozens of these orange fungi grow on the woodland floor. Carefully, I dug out a few of them to see if it really is so. Yes, it is!

Caterpillar's head

pupae

· As becomes a true toadstool, it sends millions of spores into the air. Some caterpillars eat those spores with their snack of greens. And when they crawl into the ground to

pupate, they're taken over by the toadstool. No butterfly will ever crawl out of the cocoon. Where an orange finger like that is sticking out of the ground, a tragedy has happened…

At first glance it looks like nothing more than a nice old oak tree. But there's much more to it if you take a closer look...

Rain, sun, frost and wind have made its bark perfect for nourishing all sorts of algae, mosses and lichens.

Like brother together on a branch!

And another branch full of green life.

The acorns are for the wood mice

I take a number of the branches back to my worktable. And from the warmth of the lamp, it happens:

First a small spider appears, then a little beetle, a caterpillar, another beetle and then all kinds of small insects. You can see clearly what the birds find here to satisfy their hunger.

A baby gall wasp flies out when I open an oak apple. Now he's flying around the room looking for an oak tree.

So much life around that one old tree!

At the florist, I had ordered a bouquet of flowers for a friend's birthday...
"What color would you like?" I carefully chose a combination of soft shade

An hour later, I was walking
in the woods and saw something m-u-u-uch more
exciting than that safe color combination! I never
would have dared to suggest these colors
to the lady in the flower shop!

What's rustling there in the grass?
Dung beetles, or mice?
MICE!

eauty? Oh well,
Saar ignores it.
She has
other priorities...

A hedgehog enjoys her last meal before the cold weather sets in. When she's finished, she'll find a nice place to hibernate, like under this woodpile.

I carefully dried a collection of pretty leaves in my old telephone book. They'll be nice to frame soon!

In the winter the great spotted woodpecker lives primarily on the seeds from pinecones and fir cones. But the seeds are firmly hidden among the woody scales… What to do?

With a few good blows with his beak…

he plucks the pinecone from the branch…

and flies with it to his nearest dining table

Such a place is a split or hole in a trunk which the woodpecker has carefully chiseled out to the size of a pinecone. He pushes the cone in firmly and clamps it in place. Now he can hammer the seeds out from between the scales.

One woodpecker may have dozens of these contraptions... otherwise he'd spend all his time flying back and forth! Hundreds of empty pine-cones lie underneath each one.

Ah, just back from a wonderful, tingling winter walk...Bags and hands full of things. Deeply satisfied, I lay my findings out before me.

Empty hazelnuts that were a tasty snack for the wood mice.

A branch of rowan, more fiery than ever.

A bracket fungus and a butterfly wing.

Imagine how rich you feel with such a little pile of treasures that nature could gladly spare.

Squirrels won't hibernate unless it gets very, very cold. Here she finds the food that she hid last fall.

Walking in the hushed winter forest...
but I'm not alone.

The whole time, a wren flutters around,
letting me know who's boss here.

Whipping angrily
back and forth,
he scolds me.

It sounds just like a miniature
alarm clock going off.

It's time for us to end our walk
   together, at least for now.
I know I'll be back soon
   to enjoy more of nature's wonderful
treasures that were here before me
   and that will remain long after
I've left these woods.